THAT HOLY ANARCHIST

REFLECTIONS ON CHRISTIANITY & ANARCHISM

Mark Van Steenwyk

Written by Mark Van Steenwyk

ISBN 0-6156-5981-0

*Scripture quoted by permission. All Scripture is from the NET Bible®
copyright ©1996-2006 by Biblical Studies Press, L.L.C.*

*We are using the NET Bible because we support open and free Bible
translations.* **Bible distribution should not be driven by profit
motive.**

Design by Mark Van Steenwyk

**Missio
Dei**

2717 South 8th Street
Minneapolis, MN 55406

Discounted copies available upon request.

CONTENTS

To my son Jonas
who comes by anarchism naturally
and my wife Amy
who shows me the love of Christ

"That holy anarchist who summoned the people at the bottom, the outcasts and "sinners," the chandalas within Judaism, to opposition against the dominant order—using language, if the Gospels were to be trusted, which would lead to Siberia today too—was a political criminal insofar as political criminals were possible at all in an absurdly unpolitical community. This brought him to the cross..."

Nietzsche, *the Antichrist*

A Little Preface for a Little Book

This little book grew out of a series of articles I wrote for Jesus Radicals (www.JesusRadicals.com), which in turn grew out of a primer I've presented at the annual Jesus Radicals conference. Some of the ideas were fleshed out with the help of Sarah Lynne Anderson—my friend and fellow community member at Missio Dei in Minneapolis.

There are few resources available to folks exploring the intersection of Christianity and anarchism. This is strange, given the popularity of a number of people who described themselves as both: Dorothy Day, Jacques Ellul, Simone Weil, Leo Tolstoy, Peter Maurin, and more. The resources that do exist are either academic, expensive, laboriously long, or written by long-dead Russians.

I offer this book to respond to a need. I don't assume it is either definitive or adequate. I simply offer it to spark conversation and help people dig deeper into the anarchic implications of the way of Jesus.

FORWARD

BY CHED MYERS

One of the central challenges of forging peace, justice and freedom in our time is to experiment with political models that promote the dispersal, rather than the increasing concentration, of power. This is also an ancient, if forgotten, vocation of the church.

It comes as a surprise to most contemporary Christians that the first form of social organization indigenous to the Israelites in the Hebrew Bible was a tribal confederacy that bears some resemblance to "anarcho-syndicalist" vision in modernity. It seems that ancient Yahwists exhibited a profound antagonism toward the centralized political economies and cosmologies of the Babylonian, Egyptian and Canaanite city-states in whose shadows they dwelled. This bias can be seen, for example, in the ancient folktale parodying the Tower of Babel Genesis 11, in which the social conformity of centripetal empire was deconstructed by the Creator's centrifugal "scattering" of humans into the more sustainable social ecology of diversity.

Early Israel was, as pioneer scholar Norman Gottwald famously argued, "a risky venture in 'retribalization'" in the highlands of late Bronze Age Canaan. These early Hebrew experiments in building what this booklet calls an "unkingdom" eventually succumbed to the monarchic Temple-State of David and his successors. Even during this royal period, however, the suspicion of State authority survived among both Israelite historians and prophets (see e.g. I Samuel 8). There is no other historiographic tradition ancient or modern, claimed theologian Jacques Ellul, that is as critical of centralized power as the Hebrew Bible, which articulates "in an astounding way the constancy of an antiroyal if not an antistatist sentiment." Moreover, within only a few generations, Israel's dalliance with imperial imitation led to civil war, disastrous external political alliances, and finally conquest and exile.

Jesus of Nazareth sought to resuscitate not only his people's radical tradition of the *exclusive* sovereignty of Yahweh (Mk 1:15), but the memory of the old tribal confederacy as well. Why otherwise would he organize his movement around *twelve* disciples named on a mountain (Mk 3:13-19), and specifically enjoin leadership-as-servanthood as the alternative to the prevailing politics of domination (Mk 10:42-45)? It was *this* "unking"—who embraced cross instead of sword, and who was executed as a dissident by the authorities only to defy their seal on his tomb by rising from the dead (Matt 27:64-66)—whom the early church addressed with the indivisibly political title of "Lord."

Mark Van Steenwyk is haunted by such resonances between Christianity and anarchism, and this book seeks to investigate them. Making this case seems perhaps Quixotic on the heels of more than 17 centuries of Christendom, in which churches routinely rode shotgun with empire. It is nevertheless the case that there is too much counter evidence of anarchist "tendencies" (as Van Steenwyk puts it) in both the Bible and church history to simply dismiss. This essay thus explores the intersections between these two dissident traditions.

The times, after all, demand political (and theological) imagination. Our 21st century global body politic faces the crisis, anticipated three generations ago by Lewis Mumford, of "super-congestion." With our putative democracies losing ground each year to the centripetal forces of politico-economic centralization and global technocracy, centrifugal demands for self-determination and political "devolution" are growing. The *structural* solution to over-concentrated power is to train ourselves how to organize and advocate for our concerns with the goal of radically decentralizing political decision-making —which has most recently been embodied in the Occupy movement.

In their classical statist expressions, *both* liberal capitalism and communism have anathematized the politics of local empowerment. This has led many to look instead to the 19th century revolutionary movements of cooperative socialism and anarchism. Anarchism may have peaked as a modern political force in the period between the Paris Commune of 1871 and the Spanish Civil War in the late 1930s. But there was a notable revival of anarchist ideas and tactics in the New Left movements of the 1960s, and over the last 15 years they have again captured the imagination of many First World anti-globalization and environmental activists—not to mention radical Christian groups.

I agree with those who contend that anarchism is to Marxism-Leninism what Anabaptism was to the magisterial Reformation: a revolutionary movement predicated upon *negating*, rather than *seizing control of*, state power. Just as the Anabaptists were scorned by Protestants and Catholics alike, anarchism been dismissed equally by the political Left and Right in modernity. But in our age of political bankruptcy, this is perhaps the best endorsement. With Ellul, I think that anarchism deserves to be reconsidered, particularly by Christians, and even more particularly by contemporary Anabaptists.

This booklet represents such a reconsideration. It emerges from a new generation of Christian dissenters who are properly disillusioned, but not despairing. The author is the genial pastor of an alternative urban community in Minneapolis that is affiliated with the Mennonite Church U.S., and a member of the collective behind JesusRadicals.com. I hope his overview of biblical "retribalizing politics," modern anarchism, and the concluding proposal for "Christo-anarchism" will encourage and inspire younger activists (Christian, anarchist, or both) to move beyond sloganeering to a deeper, engaged conversation at this critical intersection of faith and politics.

Jesus' last parable in Mark's gospel completes a circle of discourse opened by his first. His inaugural parable promised to "plunder" a "House" (symbolizing the Judean body politic) that was captive to the "Strong Man" (a metaphor for Empire; Mk 3:27). Mark's Jesus later "exorcised" that House (11:15-17), then called for its deconstruction (13:2). He pointedly closed his last sermon by envisioning a House in which "authority/power" (the word is the same in Greek) is distributed to a multiplicity of servants, "each with their own task" (13:34ff; Gk *dous tois doulois autou tēn exousian*).

It is an image that captures succinctly the anarchist vision —a "heresy" which may yet be a key to the renewal of church and society.

1

JESUS AND THE UNKINGDOM OF GOD

Traditional kingship (with absolute power, hoards of wealth, and power over the weak) has nothing to do with Jesus; it's something Jesus rejected.[1] Traditional kings demand allegiance and servitude, but Jesus offers liberation—from suffering, sickness and death, exclusion, persecution, and sin. Jesus is a "king" who serves the "least of these", and who finally receives torture and execution to bring freedom to others.

As we see in the Gospels, Christ's kingship is inconsistent with traditional structures of power; and for this reason, Jesus tells Pilate that "My kingdom is not from this world" (John 18:36). Passages like these have, unfortunately, fostered an ineffectual other-worldliness among Christians. And they have been used to legitimate "real-world" kingdoms. Jesus rules some magical sky-kingdom, while princes and emperors can dominate flesh and land.

But Jesus' reign isn't other-worldly. It isn't apolitical. It's just political in a radically different way. Rather than taking Caesar's throne (or any throne—including the one Satan offered him[2]) Jesus is saying that Caesar's days are numbered. By saying "my kingdom is not from this world" he isn't saying "my kingdom is only spiritual, so you don't have to worry."[3] Jesus' kingship renders Caesar's obsolete.

---

1 See John 6:15.
2 See Matthew: 4:1-11 and Luke 4:1-13
3 A number of scholars have successfully made this point. For example, N.T. Wright argues "The sentence should not be

It isn't a mere "trumping" as though Jesus is simply *greater* than Caesar; it is an entirely different sort of kingship.

As heirs to Jesus' kingdom, we are ambassadors of the new reign, privileged to share the mercy, love, peace, and justice of Christ with the world. In the early days—the first century of the Jesus movement—the church was invisible to most people in the Roman empire. However, they had a growing reputation as an alternative and seemingly anti-social community that lived in the nooks and crannies of Empire.

Christians were thought to be extreme, subversive, stubborn, and defiant. The Roman writer Tacitus called them "haters of humanity." They rejected the central facets of Roman religious and political life. In his view they actively undermined society with their indifference to civic affairs. Some critics even blamed Christians for the fall of Rome.

So, when Jesus said his kingdom wasn't of this world, he wasn't understood by Pilate or by the Jews or by his earliest followers as talking about the afterlife or some abstracted spiritual truth. Based upon the lethal response to Jesus (and the early reactions to Jesus' movement), the "Kingdom of God" was understood as a challenge to Caesar and his reign. Their two kingdoms clashed.

---

read as referring to an other-worldly, Platonic, non-physical kingdom. It designates Jesus' kingdom as the breaking into the worldly order of a rule which comes from elsewhere, from Israel's God, the creator God. It does not mean the abandonment of the created order and the escape into a private or 'spiritual' sphere. On to the scene of worldly power - precisely there, or it is meaningless! - has come a new order of sovereignty, which wins its victories by a new method." N.T. Wright, "The New Testament and the 'State'" *Themelios* 16.1 (1990): 11-17.

The kingdom of God that Jesus announced and embodied is what life would be like on earth, here and now, if God were king and the rulers of this world were not. Imagine if God ruled the nations.

But in order to imagine that, we'd need to recognize that Jesus' kingdom isn't the sort that one holds with an iron fist. Rather, it is an unkingdom.[4] Despite our images of God, I'm not sure that God is interested in either hierarchy or control. For where the President of the United States insists on a troop surge, Jesus calls people to love their enemies. Where dictators seek to secure their own power and prestige, Jesus calls people to serve one another and lay down their lives for friends. Since Jesus is (as Christians believe) the truest revelation of God, then he defines for us what the reign of God looks like.

The social, economic, political, and religious subversions of such an un-reign are almost endless—peace-making instead of war mongering, liberation not exploitation, sacrifice rather than subjugation, mercy not vengeance, care for the vulnerable instead of privileges for the powerful, generosity instead of greed, embrace rather than exclusion.

Jesus is calling for a loving anarchy. An unkingdom. Of which he is the unking.

---

4   I am indebted to my friend Jason Evans for first introducing me to the idea of seeing Jesus as an "unking."

2

This book explores the intersection of Christianity and anarchism. Most people think such a combination is an impossibility (or a delusion). But it would be a mistake to suggest that bringing the two together is mere novelty. In fact, you can trace some amazingly anarchistic sentiments throughout church history. And you can find Christians among many anarchist collectives. The relationship may be strained, but they have always been on speaking terms.

Most of the negative reactions to this interplay are based upon misunderstandings. It is commonly understood that anarchism is for angry youth who long for chaos and disorder.

And if anarchism is about chaos, Christianity is about order. Oppressive order. It is commonly understood that Christianity is (and always has been) about domination.

Both of these are unfortunate stereotypes that, while having some basis in reality, are grossly over-simplified dismissals (though, in all fairness, it is easier to find evidence for the oppressiveness of Christianity than it is for the chaotic immaturity of anarchism).

Anyone who has called themselves a "Christian" or an "anarchist" for very long can tell you that neither "tradition" is easy to define. Neither is monolithic. And both are profoundly misunderstood. So talking about how they relate is a complicated task.

Defining anarchism is problematic (to "define" something often implies the authority to do so, after all). Nevertheless, for sake of clarity, I will offer my best attempt at a reasonable definition. "An-arch" means contrary to authority or without ruler. So "anarchism" is the name given to the principle under which a collectivity —a group of people—may be conceived without rule. Specifically, anarchism is traditionally understood to be a critique of the "state" while promoting a stateless society.

That is the basic text-book definition. Most anarchists go further, trying to name those things that oppress or give the State its power and, therefore, seek to reject or undermine other forms of static authority in human relations. Some extend that beyond human relations. Furthermore, in recent years, anarchist organizing has increasingly focused on economic concerns...suggesting that there are things more powerful and oppressive than the State. Hardt and Negri[5] (and others) point out that our modern iteration of "empire" is super-national, being driven by international banking and super-corporations. It would be fair to say that anti-capitalism or anti-globalization are as important (or, perhaps, even more important) than being against the State.

At the same time, there are others who call themselves anarchists that embrace free markets. Most anarchists (rightfully) reject such "anarcho-capitalists" as not anarchist at all. Anarchist thought grew out of the same soil as Marxism. This only *hints* at the complexity of defining anarchism...which has led to a number of hyphenated terms like anarcha-feminism, anarcho-syndicalism, anarcho-communism, anarcho-primitivism,

---

5 Their book *Empire* is a significant contribution to understanding the nature of postcolonial imperialism.

post-anarchism, and so on. Different flavors represent different understandings of either the roots of oppression, the tactics for resisting oppression, or both. Most of these critiques are not mutually exclusive.

Most anarchists today aren't interested in simply subverting the State—which is, perhaps, the focus of criticism for classical anarchism. It is important to recognize the intersection of various forms of oppression. Elisabeth Schüssler Fiorenza coined the helpful term "kyriarchy" (from the Greek word *kyrios*, which can signify the domination of the emperor, lord, master, father, husband, or elite propertied male) to signify the complex inter-relatedness of various forms of oppression (like classism, sexism, racism, etc). These various forms of domination do not stand alone. Rather, they reinforce one another into a domination system.[6]

In recent years, anarcho-primitivism has gained traction as an anarchist critique of civilization as a whole. This move is important because, I believe, oppression and domination goes much deeper than a critique of the State or of corporations or of any powerful elite. Rather, it goes deeper into the fabric of our social structures. Primitivism, perhaps, attempts to name this more fully than any other "school" (for lack of a better word) of thought. However, while I believe there is much to learn from anarcho-primitivist critiques, I don't think anarcho-primitivists have been careful enough in addressing the way in which particular dominations intersect to create systemic oppression today.

I have found it helpful to focus my critique on the "empire" as a manifestation of inter-related oppressions. Empire is, in our context, that social reality (or unreality,

---

6 For more on this, see Elisabeth Schüssler Fiorenza's *The Power of the Word: Scripture and the Rhetoric of Empire.*

depending upon how you look at it) that globally reaches out to manage all of creation (including humanity) into a system of exploitation wherein only the elite ultimately benefit. It is the bringing of death to the whole of life. Anarchists are rarely simply against the State—they have (or should) become namers of all forms of oppression, seeking to understand the way oppressions reinforce each other in enslaving creation and seeing, in contrast, a way of liberation and life for all of creation.

Anarchism is, as a defined idea, a new concept. This complicates any effort to delve too deeply into the past in order to name any group or movement as "anarchist." However, as anthropologist David Graeber writes:

> The nineteenth-century "founding figures" (Bakunin, Kropotkin, and Proudhon) did not think of themselves as having invented anything particularly new. The basic principles of anarchism—self-organization, voluntary association, mutual aid—referred to forms of human behavior they assumed to have been around about as long as humanity. The same goes for the rejection of the State and of all forms of structural violence, inequality, or domination...even the assumption that all these forms are somehow related and reinforce each other. None of it was presented as some startling new doctrine. And in fact it was not: one can find records of people making similar arguments throughout history, despite the fact there is every reason to believe that in most times and places, such opinions were the ones least likely to be written down. We are talking less about a body of theory, then, than about an attitude, or perhaps one might even say a faith: the

rejection of certain types of social relations, the confidence that certain others would be much better ones on which to build a livable society, the belief that such a society could actually exist.[7]

Graeber rightly focuses on an anarchist *attitude* rather than an anarchist *body of theory*. Perhaps it would be more helpful to explore "the anarchic impulse" rather than to articulate an "ism" called "anarchism." Naming the "anarchic impulse" allows one to recognize a familiar posture without anachronistically co-opting past movements (too much). Anarchism *tends* to be praxis-oriented, rather than theoretically-oriented. Graeber suggests that we understand Marxism as a system of thought while anarchism is most at home in on-the-ground practices. At its best, anarchism isn't theoretical, with all its abstract-thought-ducks lined up in a row, but rather an evolving endeavor where thought flows out of experiment and practice. In other words, anarchism is perhaps best understood in terms of postures and practices, not as a body of theory.

It would make sense, then, that those who follow Jesus Christ (who presumably want to embody the way of love), would feel drawn to a set of practices and theories that seek to remove oppressive social relations and, instead, seek a new way of relating.

DEFINING "CHRISTIANITY"

Christianity is even harder to define. It has more adherents, a longer history, and thousands of self-defined sects. Christianity has never been monolithic. Orthodoxy

---

7 David Graeber, *Fragments of an Anarchist Anthropology* (Chicago: Prickly Paradigm Press, 2004) pp. 3-4

has been an attempt at "defining the center"–which, whether you agree with the creeds or not–is a power move. So while there are some that would privilege their tradition as the definitive expression of Christianity, I am going to resist privileging any particular tradition or set of orthodox principles. Rather, any group that claims Jesus Christ as its primary inspiration, will be, for the purposes of this book, considered "Christian."

So, while Christianity is usually broken up into three parts by dictionaries (Catholic, Orthodox, and Protestant), such divisions only work on paper. Some groups, like the Anabaptists or Quakers, often don't think of themselves as Protestant at all. Some groups are labelled as cults (like the Mormons). Some groups claim to transcend such categorization (like evangelicals). Some assume they stand apart from denominational traditions (non-denominational churches). Pentecostalism may have roots in Protestantism, but is so unique and ubiquitous that it needs to be understood in its own terms. Of course, every single one of the groups I've mentioned has its own sub-groups.

And of course, there's always someone who simply says "I don't believe in labels–I'm just a Christian"–which is essentially a nifty cop-out. An even bigger cop-out comes from those who were spiritually and socially formed in a Christian church and still hold some of those values or beliefs, yet suggest that they don't call themselves "Christian" at all. All of this is to say that the social construct of "Christianity" is an unmitigated mess. I will say this, however: any time a group or tradition within Christianity expresses the anarchist impulse, they also stress the importance of ethics in Christian identity.

Further Reading

Dave Andrews, *Christi-Anarchy: Discovering a Radical Spirituality of Compassion*, Eugene, Oregon: Wipf and Stock Publishers, 2012.

David Graeber, *Fragments of an Anarchist Anthropology,* Chicago: Prickly Paradigm Press, 2004.

Peter Marshall, *Demanding the Impossible: A History of Anarchism*, Oakland: PM Press, 2010.

3

ANARCHIC IMPULSES IN CHRISTIAN HISTORY

Christian history has a number of examples that demonstrate an anarchic impulse and their common features are revealing. For most of these groups, anarchic tendencies were intertwined with spiritual and theological convictions. Their spirituality and politics were integrated. There is something deeply lacking when we imagine a Christian anarchism that simply "slaps together" one's Christianity and one's anarchism. It is not only possible, but (I believe) necessary to have an anarchism that flows out of one's spirituality (or, perhaps, vice versa).

So, what are some expressions of Christianity that authentically express the anarchic impulse? I'll briefly examine some of those groups who demonstrate self-organization, voluntary association, mutual aid, and anti-authoritarianism.

A BRIEF SURVEY OF ANARCHIC CHRISTIAN HISTORY[8]

It is perhaps worth noting the difference between being anarchist towards government (but not the church e.g. the early Catholic Worker) and being anarchist internally (but not so much towards government e.g. Quakers). And

---

8 A number of friends protested the following survey. Orthodox friends, Lutheran friends, and Catholic friends all balked at the exclusion of their traditions from this chapter. While I acknowledge that it is possible to be an anarchist and meaningfully participate in any tradition, this isn't to say that the anarchist impulse naturally flows from those traditions.

there are some groups that approach something like anarchism both internally and externally (like the Beguines). Despite the diversity of perspectives offered, I believe the following groups each reveal something of the anarchist impulse in their own way. I have no doubt more could be added; perhaps it will inspire you in your own quest to find anarchist threads in the fabric of Christian history.

The Early Church, some argue, was anarchistic. This is, of course, a bold claim. Everyone claims that the heart of their version of Christianity is expressed by the early church. Nevertheless, some of the early Christian communities seem to have practiced certain features of anarchism.

For example, the Jerusalem group, as described in Acts, shared their money and labor equally and fairly among members. There are also indications of consensus decision making (Acts 15). Within Pauline Christianity, we see glimpses of mutual submission rather than hierarchy (Ephesians 5), a charismatic understanding of authority and power wherein spiritual authority isn't located within any one person but, instead, any person could manifest the Spirit (1 Corinthians 12-14), and a fundamental egalitarianism (Galatians 3 and Colossians 3).

Some, such as Ammon Hennacy, have claimed that a "shift" away from Jesus' practices and teachings of nonviolence, simple living, and freedom occurred in the theology of Paul of Tarsus. Hennacy (and others) suggest that Christians should look at returning to pre-"Pauline Christianity". However, if we focus on writings clearly belonging to Paul while grappling with the complexity of his context and rhetoric, we can see within the Pauline epistles something like anarchism.

Others point further down the road to the evolving relationship with the State (leading to what many call the "Constantinian Shift"). It is clear that in its earliest centuries, the Church rejected the religion, economics, and violence of empire. Often, Christians saw themselves as a distinct socio-political reality which, while not necessarily anarchistic, certainly had many similar components. This socio-political distinction eroded as Christianity gained favor in the Roman Empire.

The Bogomils were a 10th Century sect with Gnostic tendencies. They called for a return to early Christianity and, as a result, rejected church authority. They also resisted state authority. They didn't build church buildings, preferring to worship outdoors. They were dualists who saw corporeal life as a creation of the Devil. Nevertheless, their anti-materialism led them to refuse to pay taxes, to work as serfs, or to fight in wars. It is possible that the Bogomils reflected the sentiments of earlier gnostic groups whose socio-political views have been obscured.

Beguines and the Beghards were lay orders of women and men in the 12th to 14th centuries. They often lived a monastic lifestyle together without formally taking vows. Communities were autonomous, largely egalitarian, and often challenged class distinctions. They found themselves in trouble with both the Church and the State, since the Beguines and Beghards often did things according to their own communal discernment. Many influential Beguines believed in an unmediated mystical connection with God, thus rendering the structures of the Church (and therefore the State) largely inconsequential.

The Lollards—followers of John Wycliffe who were deemed heretics and extremists—had anti-authoritarian tendencies that flowed from their understanding of the Gospel. Their movement began in the mid 14th century and continued into the Reformation. In their document *the Twelve Conclusions of the Lollards* (penned in 1396-1397), they rejected papal authority, challenged the political collusion of State and Church, and undermined the legitimacy of war.

The Anabaptists (the radical reformers of the 16th Century) initially lived autonomously with indifference to secular government. And, while largely patriarchal, such groups practiced a sort of egalitarianism that didn't invest authority into any one individual. Through the ages some of this indifference has eroded (though, thankfully, so has much of its patriarchalism). In his essay on anarchism for the *Encyclopedia Britannica*, Peter Kropotkin traces the birth of anarchist thought in Europe to early Anabaptist communities. This makes sense, since traditional Anabaptists separated themselves from the functions and practices of the State. In addition, Anabaptists past and present have generally embraced pacifism and some groups have held property in common.

The Quakers (Society of Friends) formed in the 17th century. The Quakers are internally organized along anarchist lines. All decisions are made locally and by consensus (which has had a tremendous influence on modern anarchist decision making) and are largely egalitarian. While Quakers don't usually bring this approach into an anarchist political theory, Quaker approaches to power and violence has led to significant cross-pollination between Christian anarchists and Quakers.

The Diggers were a 17th century group of agrarian communists in England. They believed in holding land in common in small egalitarian rural communities. Founder of the movement, Gerrard Winstanley argued in his 1649 pamphlet *Truth Lifting up its Head above Scandals* that power corrupts, that property enslaves, and that freedom is only possible in a society without rulers. They were deeply influenced by the example given in the early chapters of Acts. The Diggers are a fascinating example of how the communist impulses of the early church inspired a communist agrarianism that, in turn, nurtured anarchistic understandings of authority. With the Diggers, spirituality shaped economics, which in turn, shaped political understandings.

The Dukhobors are a Russian group of unknown origins (though they probably emerged in the 17th Century). They continue to exist primarily in Canada. The Dukhobors reject secular government, Russian Orthodoxy, the supreme authority of Scripture, and the divinity of Jesus. Their spirituality is, like many Quakers, based upon the assumption that true spirituality is unmediated, thus rendering any mediative structures unnecessary.

The Tolstoyans are followers of the philosophical and religious views of Russian novelist Leo Tolstoy (1828–1910). They put particular emphasis on the Sermon on the Mount and other teachings of Jesus as a guide for life. Many self-identify as Christians, though in a departure from some other forms of Christianity, they tend to focus more on the teachings of Jesus as a divinely-guided human rather than the Son of God. They do not participate in, or concern themselves with, governmental and worldly affairs, which they consider immoral and corrupt. Thus, they may be described as anarchists, though not all of them claim that title. They embrace a deep pacifism–often refusing to defend themselves. Many are vegetarian or vegan. Tolstoy influenced Gandhi (and his understanding of nonviolence) and European anarchism. It is important to note that Kropotkin recognized Christian anarchism (as developed by Tolstoy) as one of four strands of anarchism in his day (early

1900s). The other strands are anarcho-communism, Proudhonism, and literary-anarchism.

The Catholic Workers (particularly its founders) have found common ground between a relatively "conservative" reading of Scripture and political anarchism. Begining in the early to mid 20th century, the workers center around the practice of the works of mercy, a belief in personalism, and living communally in either houses of hospitality or farming communes. The workers are involved in anti-war and anti-nuclear resistance and, in recent years, have become increasingly active in anti-globalization work.

Liberation Theology in general, and the Ecclesial Base Communities in particular, are not anarchist per se, but within this movement, there has been a huge re-imagining of the authority of Church and of the State. Most liberationists seem to have a clear socialist bent, but there are anarchist sparks here and there. Some early liberationists drew inspiration from folks like Dorothy Day (co-founder of the Catholic Worker) and Tolstoy. While the influence of Marxist thought has been well researched, little attention has been given to the anarchist influences within Liberation Theology.[9] Nevertheless, for many Christian anarchists, liberation theology has provided the most fertile intellectual soil for growing a faith that integrates spirituality and political thought.

There are, of course, other groups worth mentioning. Many have been influenced by those movements that touch on an aspect of anarchist thought—like Francis' approach to wealth, Wesley's way of organizing small groups of faith and practice, the monastic approach to

---

9 For an example of a work that does examine this relationship, see Linda H. Damico's *The Anarchist Dimension of Liberation Theology.*

common life and mutuality, etc.[10]

CHRISTIAN ANARCHIST EXPRESSIONS TODAY

While many Christian anarchists I've met have been conversant with the movements listed, few have emerged from these groups. I've met Christian anarchists who join the Catholic Worker, become Mennonite (like myself), or participate in a Quaker meeting. But, for the most part, contemporary Christian anarchists emerge out of decidedly mainstream Christian circles and become radicalized towards anarchism.

Many Christian anarchists were first introduced to anarchistic ideas through engagement with a Catholic Worker community or Christian intentional community. Others found their way to Christian anarchism through books which either articulate a Christian Anarchist perspective (or come close). Writers such as Dorothy Day, Jacques Ellul, John Howard Yoder, Greg Boyd, or Shane Claiborne have wooed many into an anarchist perspective. In my own context (North America), the strongest network for Christian anarchism remains the Catholic Worker movement. In addition to the Catholic Worker movement, Jesus Radicals has played a role in networking and gathering Christian anarchists (primarily in the United States). Other notable networks or gatherings that have been somewhat friendly to North American Christian anarchism have been Papa Fest and the

---

10 Any groups demonstrating a tendency towards anti-authoritarians were likely to be suppressed, making ancient and early medieval sources particularly difficult to find. Earlier reviewers advocated for the inclusion of the Celtic Christians, Donatists, and more. Early "heretical" groups were cast off for more than theological reasons; the particularities of their dissent have often been obscured by suppression.

communities associated with the New Monasticism. By all accounts, Christian anarchism is on the rise. However, it isn't gathering around a popular figure, organization, or movement. That is, in many ways, how it should be (though more organizing certainly needs to be done).

LESSONS LEARNED

So, what can we learn from this stroll through history? How does it inform our own lives in this season? I confess that I bring my own agenda to this history lesson. No doubt you can draw out some lessons of your own. Nevertheless, here are are seven issues I'd like to raise from this brief history lesson:

1) Every single one of the groups listed has been considered heretical, in some way, by the dominant religious groups of their time. This may seem obvious, but if a religious group is dominant, they won't like anti-authoritarian tendencies among its religious adherents. Given this history, we shouldn't expect mainstream Christianity to naturally shift towards anarchism.

2) Many of these groups are "heretical" (or at least flirted with "heresy") in more than one area. If we are intellectually honest, our anarchist impulses will affect more than simply our view of the government. The anarchist impulse causes us to rethink every relationship, including our relationships with spiritual authority (which may also include the Bible, Jesus, and God). That doesn't mean we have to open up the doors of every classical "heresy". It does, however, suggest that the anarchic impulse doesn't play safely with every expression of mainstream Christianity. When a belief is deemed a "heresy" it often accompanies the marginalizing of a group of people who have gathered around that belief. It is difficult to discern whether the group is ostracized

because it is heretical, or deemed heretical because it is a beneficial tactic of the dominant group to eliminate a threat.

3) Most radical Christian groups either die out or go mainstream. We should try to learn from those groups that still exist but haven't mainstreamed. They may hold keys to sustainable nonconformity.

4) You'll notice a large gap from the early church to the Bogomils. This doesn't mean that there were no Christians with anarchist impulses between the 4th and 10th centuries. It is likely that many "heretical" groups (Novations, Donatists, Pelagians, etc.) or early monastic expressions could have made the list. However, there isn't as much information about fringe groups during those centuries. What we do know about these groups is largely offered by their religious/political enemies. This isn't to say that all such groups were nifty and worthy of emulation. However, we simply do not know how much such groups could inspire us in our own messy efforts to live faithfully in the midst of civilization.

5) While some groups influenced later groups, there isn't a successive chain of radical Christianity. The anarchic impulse isn't passed down through the ages like a baton. Rather, it emerges and re-emerges. I believe that the Spirit of God creates anarchy. We should, perhaps, be open to new expressions of the anarchic impulse emerging from unexpected places. This should be cause for hope: even in the most unlikely of places, life breaks out like a weed sprouting through a crack in a sidewalk.

6) Most movements mentioned above had early founders and influencers who were mystics. In her work *The Silent Cry*, Dorothee Soelle points to the mystical nature of liberation. We would be wise to ground our anarchism in a real mysticism—one that embraces a sort of divine

wildness that can empower us to love in an unloving world. One that gives us a glimpse of a reality that we can't yet see. That mysticism can be linked to anarchism makes sense: mystics often reject the notion that access to God is mediated.

7) While it may seem unnecessary in our media age, it is important that we pass along our wisdom to the next generations. Even in my lifetime I've seen a communication gap between older radicals and folks in my generation (or younger). We need to learn how to share our best insights. We need to become evangelists in ways that subvert efforts at suppression.

Further Reading

Andrew Bradstock and Christopher Rowland, *Radical Christian Writings: A Reader,* Oxford: Blackwell Publishers, 2001.

Alexandre Christoyannopoulos, *Christian Anarchism: A Political Commentary on the Gospel,* Exeter: Imprint Academic, 2011.

Linda H. Damico, *The Anarchist Dimension of Liberation Theology,* New York: Peter Lang Publishing, 1987.

Dorothy Day, *Loaves and Fishes,* Maryknoll, New York: Orbis Books, 1963.

Jacques Ellul, *Anarchy and Christianity*, Eugene, Oregon: Wipf and Stock Publishers, 2011.

Leo Tolstoy, *The Kingdom of God is Within You,* Maryknoll, New York: Orbis Books, 2006.

Tripp York, *Living on Hope While Living in Babylon: The Christian Anarchists of the Twentieth Century*, Eugene, Oregon: Wipf and Stock Publishers, 2009.

4

ANARCHIC IMPULSES IN SCRIPTURE

For most Christians, there is one big reason for rejecting anarchism: it isn't biblical. Or is it? A superficial reading of the Bible reveals a God who thinks of *him*self as a sort of Warrior King, who sanctions state-enacted genocide, and who promotes a string of saintly kings, like King David. When Jesus arrives, it is to start a Kingdom of God that, apparently, seems content to co-exist with earthly rulership. In fact, Jesus himself says to "render to Caesar what is Caesar's" and Paul advocates being good subjects to the governing authorities. Therefore, Christian anarchism is a contradiction in terms, right?

Furthermore, the sorts of ideas many Christian anarchists hold are also glaringly unbiblical. Like nonviolence (many biblical heroes were prolific smiters). Like communism (certain patriarchs were "blessed" with vast property– which they didn't share equally with all). Like egalitarianism (Paul tends to affirm male leadership, Jesus praises a Centurion who holds a position of authority, etc.). The Bible is the enemy of anarchism. Right?

I don't think so. While it is outside the scope of a single chapter (or book) to tackle *every* challenge that traditional readers of Scripture advance against anarchism, I can offer a short overview to serve as a simple lens for seeing Scripture differently. I'll try to note other resources for those of you who'd like to dig deeper. To really address the myriad of issues that emerge from an anarchic reading of Scripture, one would be better served by a commentary series. What I'm offering here is a super simple overview, not a complete survey. If any Bible scholars out there want to publish an *Anarchist Bible Commentary*, I would not only be happy to buy a set, but also would have great ideas for who should contribute.

THE HEBREW SCRIPTURES

Let's start at the beginning. Many read Genesis as an anti-civilizational text. It begins with the story of humans living in harmony with nature and upholds that as a pristine ideal.

As Ched Myers suggests,

> ...in the "primeval history" of Gen 1-11 Israel's sages—redacting older sources and probably writing in the aftermath of the failed monarchy—also attempt to explain [the rupture from primal life]. Eden can be interpreted as a mythic memory of the old symbiotic lifeways: humans, creatures and God dwell intimately and richly together (Gen 2).[11]

When paradise is lost, humans are relegated to hard agricultural toil.

The first act of violence is committed by the agriculturalist (Cain) rather than the nomadic herdsman (Abel). As we know, agriculture emerges with the advent of civilization. It is this murderer who establishes the first city. Later, as humanity "progresses" all sorts of crazy things happen,

---

11 read more of Ched's thoughts on the "Fall" here: http://www.chedmyers.org/system/files/The%20Fall%20-%20Anarcho%20Primitivism%20%2526%20the%20Bible.pdf

like when human population spikes, the "sons of elohim" have sex with women, people become increasingly wicked, and God sends a flood to reboot creation. Later, when folks gather to build a huge tower that reaches to the heavens, God scatters the people. For the most part, Genesis is remarkably negative about the civilizational project and its subsequent imperializing tendencies. God even has to drown the earth to knock back the evils of civilization.

Again, Myers writes:

> The "Fall" in Gen 1-11, then, is not so much a cosmic moment of moral failure as it is a progressive 'history' of decline into civilization —exactly contrary to the Myth of Progress. The biblical primeval history thus should be considered not only as "mythic memory," but also as perhaps the first literature of resistance to the grand project of civilization— rightly warning against its social pathologies and ecocidal consequences.[12]

The rest of Genesis follows the story of the first patriarchs, who YHWH has called out to become a people who will follow YHWH into a promised land. Throughout Genesis, trouble happens when the Jews favorably interact with imperial powers or try to settle too soon. While it is true that the patriarchs had many possessions, it is a stretch to infer from their wealth modern notions of property rights. Pre-agricultural nomadic peoples were tribal. While the patriarchs were hardly egalitarian, their understanding of ownership was much more communal than modern Western notions. The wealth of the tribe or clan or family was for the benefit of all. And, it would

---

12 From Ched Myers article "the Fall" in *The Encyclopdia of Religion and Nature*

seem, that God's vision for Jubilee[13] would push the communality of goods and lands even further.

Exodus tells the story of a people enslaved by the Egyptian empire and how YHWH delivers them. You know the story: YHWH calls Moses (in the burning bush theophany) to lead the Israelites out of slavery into a Promised Land. Of course, once they are liberated, the people grumble and complain–desiring a return to Egypt instead of the long journey in the wilderness. In Exodus, we see a "story of Israel's communal bonding around the mountain at which they encounter YHWH, with no need for 'sacrifice' of animals or enemies."[14] As a result of their grumbling, YHWH keeps them in the wilderness for forty years.

Then, apparently, Moses passes the mantle of leadership to Joshua—a sort of military hero who engages in war against the indigenous peoples of Canaan.[15] The people successfully settle and are attacked by their neighbors, leading YHWH to raise up "judges" to lead the people in combat against the enemies of Israel.

---

13 Every seventh year was a Sabbatical Year, during which the land is to lie fallow and agricultural activity is to cease. At the end of the year, all debts are to be forgiven. The year at the end of seven Sabbatical cycles is the year of Jubilee. At that time all land was to be redistributed back to its original owner. If these practices were kept (along with the additional stipulations to provide for aliens, widows, and others), there would be little room for economic injustice.

14 Wes Howard-Brook, *Come Out My People* (Maryknoll: NY: Orbis Books, 2012) p. 196

15 This part of Israel's history is particularly troubling. Wes Howard-Brook (and others) suggest that there are two competing irreconcilable theologies in the Hebrew Scriptures—an imperial "Zion theology" and a creation-affirming "Sinai Theology." Such scholars argue that the conquest of Canaan represents Zion theology used to legitimize the monarchy.

YHWH sets up a brilliant economic and political reality, which will follow Jubilee economic practices and, instead of having a centralized government, will employ temporary leadership as need arises. Instead of a king, God dwells among them to rule directly rather than ruling through kings or priests. For example, one of the leaders who emerges, Gideon, tells the people "I will not rule over you, nor will my son rule over you. The LORD will rule over you."[16] Unfortunately, Gideon's offspring attempt to set up a dynasty.

The people keep complaining for a king, and eventually YHWH relents. Saul—who fits the people's idea of a king—sucks. He dies in battle and David (after some oft-told bible stories transpire), becomes king. The kingdom splits during the time of David's grandson. Conflicts between the prophets and the kings become common place as Israel becomes increasingly like its neighbors, leading to the eventual demise and captivity of both the northern and southern kingdoms.

This story—from Exodus to the monarchy—is one of centralization and waywardness. As Wes Howard-Brook writes,

> As it stands in its canonical order, the story conveys a relatively (and deceivingly) simple message: the shift from a twelve tribe confederacy under YHWH's rule to a human monarchy "like the nations" (1 Sam. 8:5) was a disastrous betrayal of the unique status of Israel as YHWH's "chosen people"...Israel "converted" from the religion of creation to the religion of empire, with predictable results.[17]

---

16 Judges 8:23
17 Howard-Brook, p. 95

It is important to highlight some of what makes this a "deceivingly" simple message. It is simplistic and foolish to assume that the days of David and Solomon, with a monarchy centralized in Jerusalem and worship centralized in a Temple in Zion, should be considered a golden age. There is, according to Howard-Brook, a tension (or out-right contradiction) between the pro-monarchic "'Zion theology' that placed YHWH in the Jerusalem temple" where Solomon "could be understood as truly empowered by YHWH with 'wisdom'" and the prophetic "Sinai theology" where "Solomon's 'experience' can be written off as either wishful thinking or simply as propaganda."[18] In other words, the Hebrew Scriptures present a sort of argument between the religion of Empire (where a faithful, powerful, secure, wealthy and vast nation is centralized in Jerusalem, where YHWH and king dwell) and the religion of Creation (where a faithful people live in Jubilee, encounter YHWH in creation and amidst people, and live as kin without an earthly ruler).

As we read through the prophets, when God speaks, it is usually through a prophet who challenges the king's power and who stands outside of the machines of the monarchy. So much could be said here. The emphases of the kings are very different than those of the prophets. It is astonishing how much the prophets link idolatry and exploitation of the poor. The kings often centralize wealth and power. The prophets challenge that trend. The prophets, it would seem, still hold God's Jubilee vision in their imaginations.

One of my favorite proto-anarchist sections from the Hebrew Scriptures is Ezekiel 34. God judges the "shepherds" or rulers of Israel, essentially striking them down to become the people's sole Shepherd. Incidentally, this may be the passage that Jesus had in mind in his

---

18 Ibid., p. 132

"sheep and goats" story in Matthew 25. Here's a choice quote:

> I myself will feed my sheep and I myself will make them lie down, declares the sovereign Lord. I will seek the lost and bring back the strays; I will bandage the injured and strengthen the sick, but the fat and the strong I will destroy. I will feed them—with judgment![19]

THE NEW TESTAMENT

Let's jump right into the origin story. Luke tells the story of Jesus birth. Jesus' mother, while Jesus was still in the womb, said the following words while filled with the Spirit:

> [God] has demonstrated power with [God's] arm; [God] has scattered those whose pride wells up from the sheer arrogance of their hearts. [God] has brought down the mighty from their thrones, and has lifted up those of lowly position; [God] has filled the hungry with good things, and has sent the rich away empty.[20]

Jesus grows up. He starts his ministry and is tempted by the devil in the wilderness.[21] The temptation of Jesus by the devil reveals the manner in which Jesus understands his authority. Jesus' sense of authority bears little to no similarity to kingly authority. In the wilderness, he is tempted politically, economically, and religiously to assert his messiah-ship. But he refuses. The diabolical nature of

---

19 Ezekiel 34:15-16
20 Luke 1:51-53
21 Luke 4

his temptation isn't due to the source of the temptation— that the offer of political, economic, and religious power comes from the devil instead of God. Rather, the temptation concerns the sort of reign Jesus should pursue.[22] Jesus is the unking.

Later in Luke 4, right after his trial and baptism, Jesus goes to his home town (Nazareth) and gives a political manifesto of liberation for the poor and oppressed, essentially announcing his messiah-ship and the coming of Jubilee (the "year of the Lord's favor"). Provocatively, Jesus seems willing to include oppressors in the kingdom.[23] Which is why his hometown folks—who most likely knew him well—try to kill him.

Just to jump ahead a bit, in Luke 17:21 Jesus says (in words that would later inspire the development of Leo Tolstoy's anarchism): "The kingdom of God is within you" (or among you). In the context, it seems to be a way of suggesting that the kingdom of God isn't a place, a demonstrative regime change, or a clear event. Rather it is here. Now.

Later, when Jesus heard his friends arguing amongst themselves the pecking-order in this kingdom,[24] he tells them: "The kings of the Gentiles lord it over them, and those who exercise authority over them call themselves Benefactors. But you are not to be like that. Instead, the greatest among you should be like the youngest, and the one who rules like the one who serves." Jesus is asking his

---

22 John Howard Yoder's *The Politics of Jesus* does an excellent job developing this argument.
23 The context makes this clear. The miracles Jesus references in his sermon involve the healing of Gentiles. Furthermore, when quoting Isaiah 61, he omits the portion that speaks of "the year of the Lord's vengeance" which was understood to refer to vengeance against the Gentile oppressors of Israel.
24 Luke 22:25-26

friends to rethink everything they know about socio-political realities.

The next time you read the Gospel of Luke, try to read it through the lens of Jubilee—where the ones who have accumulated have to give up and the ones who have lost receive. Jesus tells the rich young ruler to sell everything and give it to the poor.[25] He says the same thing to his disciples, by the way.[26]

In case you think only Luke is quotable for anarchists, the Gospel of John is also pretty juicy. For example, Jesus calls Satan the "prince of the world" which is likely a way of referring to the Roman Empire.[27]

In John 18:36, in a conversation with Pilate, we learn that Jesus' kingdom is not of this world. Actually, it is perhaps better translated as "not from this world." Usually, this is interpreted as saying that Jesus' kingdom is spiritual or heavenly. However, the way such dualistic language worked in that time makes such a meaning unlikely. Rather, Jesus is saying his kingdom is different. It is something entirely new. It is a gift from God—it comes from God.

After the resurrection, we read of an account of civil disobedience in Acts 5. When the disciples were ordered by authorities to stop their teaching, they answer: "We must obey God rather than any human authority." Here's what most people hear when they read that: "We must obey God rather than any human authority in those rare circumstances where there is a clear and obvious

---

25 Luke 18:18-30
26 Luke 12:13-34 is one of the most compelling economic passages in the entire Bible. I reference it here because many people assume that the call to redistribute wealth to the poor is only made to the rich young ruler in Luke 18. It is a more common theme than that, particularly in Luke's gospel.
27 see John 12:31, 14:30, 16:11

contradiction between what the law says and God says, since God's laws trump human laws." I'm not so sure. If you believed that your messiah was a socio-political/religious unking who died and then rose from the dead (and then mystically poured his Spirit out upon you), then you might simply mean "we must obey God, not any human authority."

This helps us understand the way in which the early church practiced community. They were encouraged, among other things, to work out their issues internally rather than appealing to the courts.[28] In Romans 12, Paul argues that his friends in Rome should "not be conformed to this present world [read: empire], but be transformed by the renewing of your mind, so that you may test and approve what is the will of God." This is, again, often read as a call to be spiritual or heavenly minded. But, given the larger context, it is perhaps better to see it as a challenge to stop being so Roman-ish and, instead, pursue the way of love.

I am often asked to justify my anti-imperial reading of the New Testament. After all, the word "empire" doesn't appear in the New Testament. Well. Here's the thing. The early church was sneaky. They didn't want to sound overtly treasonous. So usually we have to try to inhabit their context with our imaginations to see Rome closer to they way they saw it. And no writing is as anti-imperial as, perhaps, John's Revelation. Read Revelation 13, 14, and 17 for a not-so subtle picture of oppressive Rome.

BUT WHAT ABOUT...?

There remain many open questions. My point here isn't so much to defend an anarchic read of Scripture as much as

---

28 1 Corinthians 6:1-6

it is to give a sketch of the possibilities. We read Scripture in ways that support authoritarianism because we learned how to read Scripture in authoritarian contexts. Once you start pulling the loose threads, you begin to find the whole authoritarian fabric unravelling. For sake of brevity, I'll address the two most commonly raised passages against Christian anarchism.

The first is Romans 13, where Paul tells his readers to "submit to the governing authorities":

> Let every person be subject to the governing authorities. For there is no authority except by God's appointment, and the authorities that exist have been instituted by God. So the person who resists such authority resists the ordinance of God, and those who resist will incur judgment (for rulers cause no fear for good conduct but for bad). Do you desire not to fear authority? Do good and you will receive its commendation, for it is God's servant for your good. But if you do wrong, be in fear, for it does not bear the sword in vain. It is God's servant to administer retribution on the wrongdoer. Therefore it is necessary to be in subjection, not only because of the wrath of the authorities but also because of your conscience. For this reason you also pay taxes, for the authorities are God's servants devoted to governing. Pay everyone what is owed: taxes to whom taxes are due, revenue to whom revenue is due, respect to whom respect is due, honor to whom honor is due.[29]

When interpretting this passage, there are several things that one must keep in mind:

---

29 Romans 13:1-7

1) This passage occurs immediately after Romans 12, where Paul challenges his readers to bless persecutors, live peaceably, never avenge, feed enemies, and overcome evil with good. By clear implication, the "governing authorities" are persecuting enemies whose evil needs to be overcome with good. Given that Paul is likely drawing directly from Jesus' teachings, it may be best to interpret the call to "be subject" as an application of the call to "turn the other cheek." It is not a call to mere obedience or happy citizenship.

2) Jacques Ellul suggests "the passage thus counsels nonrevolution, but in so doing, by that very fact, it also teaches the intrinsic nonlegitimacy of institutions."[30] In other words, the very fact that Paul has to argue, in light of enemy-love, that the people should forsake (violent) resistance reveals that the "governing authorities" are, in some sense, worthy of revolt. Just like Jesus' call to turn the other cheek recognizes that, under normal circumstances, one would hit back. To refrain from violence is a testimony to the the Roman Christian's goodness, not the goodness of Rome.

3) John Howard Yoder (and others) have (rightly) challenged translating the Greek word *tasso* as "instituted." Rather, Yoder argues that a better translation would be that the authorities are "restrained" by God. Therefore, Paul could be advising his readers against revolt since God is already restraining the rulers.[31]

4) Due to the nature of translation and the dualism in our modern imaginations (separating spiritual from political realms), we don't often recognize that Paul's language around the "powers" blurs the distinction between

---

30 Jacques Ellul, *Anarchy and Christianity* (Grand Rapids: Eerdmans, 1988), p. 88
31 See chapter ten of John Howard Yoder's *The Politics of Jesus*

political and spiritual realities. When we read words like "authorities" or "rulers" or "powers," Paul may be talking primarily about spiritual realities, political realities, or (most likely) both at the same time. This adds complexity to what would otherwise seem like a straight-forward challenge to be "subject" to the "authorities" because, elsewhere, such "authorities" are seen as enemies to Christ.

5) It is a mistake to take Romans 13 as a universal message of how Christians everywhere ought to relate to government. Wes Howard-Brook states:

> We can say, though, that whatever Paul meant to convey to the Christians at Rome in the 50s, it was not a general principle of subservience to imperial authority...we've seen how Paul's letters regularly insist on attributing to Jesus titles and authority that his audience would certainly have heard as "plagiarized" from Roman sources...The most likely explanation of Romans 13 is that it was a message addressed to specific concerns of Roman Christians under Nero.[32]

And so, from Paul's perspective, the Christians in Rome in the 50s should not revolt. Rather, they should love their oppressors and leave wrath to God. This wasn't because the Roman government was good, but because followers of Jesus are called to the way of love. Furthermore, God has restrained the authorities and will judge them.

Much more could be said about what such teachings could mean for us. At the very least, it encourages us to trust God and love our enemies. While Paul argues against violent resistance, his words leave room for nonviolent struggle. It would be foolish, I think, to extrapolate

---

32 Howard-Brook, p. 464

universal principles of governmental engagement from this passage. Nevertheless, once we understand Paul's sentiments, we can better discern how to express the love of God in our own contexts.

Tied for the most referenced anti-anarchy passage is Mark 12:13-17:

> Then they sent some of the Pharisees and Herodians to trap him with his own words. When they came they said to him, "Teacher, we know that you are truthful and do not court anyone's favor, because you show no partiality but teach the way of God in accordance with the truth. Is it right to pay taxes to Caesar or not? Should we pay or shouldn't we?" But he saw through their hypocrisy and said to them, "Why are you testing me? Bring me a denarius and let me look at it." So they brought one, and he said to them, "Whose image is this, and whose inscription?" They replied, "Caesar's." Then Jesus said to them, "Give to Caesar the things that are Caesar's, and to God the things that are God's." And they were utterly amazed at him.

Clearly they were trying to trick Jesus into publicly picking sides—either would be dangerous. If he sided with Rome, he'd lose the support of the people. If he denounced Rome, he'd be a marked man. The fact that Herodians and Pharisees are working together against Jesus is telling; Jesus is so offensive that enemies have put aside their differences to resist him. What is remarkable about this passage isn't so much that Jesus is clever. The implications of his statement are remarkable.

Are the implications that we should be Augustinian, creating a distinction between church and state? Or even separating them into two separate kingdoms with different claims as Luther or some Anabaptists have advocated? No. This is a very smart slap against Caesar without simply denouncing Caesar. By pointing to their coin (no good Jew should have a graven image like a coin in their pocket to begin with), Jesus is exposing idolatry and saying that such things belong to Caesar already, not God. If you've got any Caesar-stuff, it should be rendered accordingly. But what is God's belongs to God. Or, to quote Dorothy Day, "If we rendered unto God all the things that belong to God, there would be nothing left for Caesar."

Lest you think that such approaches to scripture are a recent innovation, I direct you to Irenaeus. Irenaeus was a 2nd Century bishop on the fringes of the Empire in Lugdunum, Gaul. He was a disciple of Polycarp, who was a disciple of the Apostle John. In other words, he was removed from Jesus by two generations; he was a friend of a friend of Jesus:

> The Lord himself directed us to "render unto Caesar the things which are Caesar's, and to God the things which are God's," naming Caesar as Caesar, but confessing God as God. In like manner also, that which says, "You cannot serve two masters," he does himself interpret, saying "You cannot serve God and mammon," acknowledging God as God, but mentioning mammon, a thing also having an existence. He does not call mammon Lord when he says, "You cannot serve two masters," but he teaches his disciples who serve God,

not to be subject to mammon nor to be ruled by it...[33]

In other words, Irenaeus believed that the thing we should render Caesar is our renunciation. Caesar's lordship is comparable to that of mammon[34]. He is only your lord if you are his slave.

---

33 Irenaeus, *Against Heresies*, 3.8.1

34 Mammon is more than mere "money." It is likely that Jesus (and the early church) thought of Mammon as something demonic. "Mammon" not only signified money or wealth, but the entire economic system of exploitation. By the Middle Ages, many conceived of Mammon as the arch-demon of greed.

Further Reading

Wes Howard-Brook, *Come Out My People,* Maryknoll, New York: Orbis Books, 2012.

Norman Gottwald, Tribes of Yahweh: A Sociology of the Religion of Liberated Israel, 1250-1050 BCE, Sheffield: Sheffield Academic Press, 1999.

Ched Myers, *Binding the Strongman, A Political Reading of Mark's Gospel,* Maryknoll, New York: Orbis Books, 1988.

John Howard Yoder, *The Politics of Jesus*, Grand Rapids: Eerdmans, 1994.

5

TENSIONS

In writing this little book (where I've oh-so-briefly explored the complementarity of the way of Jesus and anarchism and the way the anarchic impulse has been expressed in Christian scriptures and history), I've realized a few things. Firstly, so much more work needs to be done.

Secondly, no matter how sophisticated or compelling one's arguments, people have always (and will always) declare with certainty that anarchism and Christianity are fundamentally incompatible. Let me give a classic example. Someone reposted a digital version of chapter one on anarchistnews.org. Predictably, many comments reflected this sentiment:

> What's anarchistic with worshipping and serving a man, anyways? Socialist perhaps... fascistic, absolutely.

Many anarchists I know assume that, at best, Christian anarchists are either anarchists who refuse to let go of their childhood fantasies or Christians who really don't understand anarchism. I suspect that their suspicions are often correct.

Anarchism, particularly as a loose set of principles, doesn't often "play well" with Christianity. For one to be a Christian anarchist, one would be considered fringe by the vast majority of Christians in history. But one would also be considered fringe by most anarchists as well. After all, "no gods, no masters" is a well-embraced slogan by many —if not most—anarchists.

According to the *Anarchist FAQ:*

> So there is a minority tradition within anarchism which draws anarchist conclusions from religion. However, as we noted in section A.2.20, most anarchists disagree, arguing that anarchism implies atheism and it is no coincidence that biblical thought has, historically, been associated with hierarchy and defense of earthly rulers. Thus the vast majority of anarchists have been and are atheists, for "to worship or revere any being, natural or supernatural, will always be a form of self-subjugation and servitude that will give rise to social domination. As [Bookchin] writes: 'The moment that human beings fall on their knees before anything that is 'higher' than themselves, hierarchy will have made its first triumph over freedom.'"

> ...Clearly, a Christian anarchist would have to be as highly selective as non-anarchist believers when it comes to applying the teachings of the Bible...if non-anarchist believers are to be considered as ignoring the teachings of the Bible by anarchist ones, the same can be said of them by those they attack...

> Moreover the idea that Christianity is basically anarchism is hard to reconcile with its history. The Bible has been used to defend injustice far more than it has been to combat it. In countries where Churches hold de facto political power, such as in Ireland, in parts of

South America, in nineteenth and early twentieth century Spain and so forth, typically anarchists are strongly anti-religious because the Church has the power to suppress dissent and class struggle. Thus the actual role of the Church belies the claim that the Bible is an anarchist text.[35]

Before I dig in, I want to raise, as honestly as possible, some of the challenges in pairing "Christianity" with "anarchism." I'm not talking about the obvious ones that your gun-toting baptist uncle would tell you. I'm talking about the tensions that arise between Christian anarchists and "secular" anarchists. This isn't an exhaustive list, but they are the ones I hear most often.

Religion is based upon domination...

Sure. Some definitions of religion assume a controlling dominant God. Furthermore, most definitions and expressions of religion also assume social structures and hierarchies that most anarchists reject. Christian anarchists usually get at this in one of two ways: a) They say the anarchist critique doesn't apply to God and God-ordained systems...that anarchism is only about "man-made" things. b) They suggest that it is possible to hold communally shared spiritual beliefs and practices and stories without affirming social hierarchies and authority (as typically defined).

I fall into that second category. I don't believe that it makes any sense to say "God is such a big King that he obliterates all other kings...therefore, I'm an anarchist." Rather, I would say "The way in which God sustains and

---

35 See section A.3.7 of the *Anarchist FAQ,* which is available at infoshop.org.

shapes existence...and calls us to be in deeper relationship is the opposite of how Kings function...therefore, I am an anarchist." To quote the late Dorothee Soelle:

> Obedience presupposes duality: one who speaks and one who listens; one who knows and one who is ignorant; a ruler and ruled ones. Religious groups who broke away from the spirit of dependency and obedience cherish different values such as mutuality and interdependence...The main virtue of an authoritarian religion is obedience...God's love and righteousness are less important than God's power...why do people worship a God whose supreme quality is power, not justice; whose interest lies in subjection, not in mutuality; who fears equality?"[36]

Jesus is an unking. To me, this doesn't simply mean he is not a king. Rather, he is the king who subverts kingship. He isn't simply the opposite of a king, rather, he is something far deeper—he transcends and excludes kingship. I worship the one who calls me friend. But I don't think it would be accurate to say that I "obey" him in the way that servants obey masters. That is just a first step–a metaphor. Just as most green anarchists believe they should respect, cherish, and affirm nature, I am called to worship and love the source of life. Semantics? Not to me.

Christianity affirms submission...

What do we do about the very clear language of discipleship and submission in the New Testament? I've

36 Dorothee Soelle, *Beyond Mere Obedience* (New York: The Pilgrim Press, 1982), xiii-xiv

already explored the anarchist impulse in the New Testament, so I'm not going to argue about whether or not the New Testament supports social hierarchies (I think some of it does, and some of it doesn't–but I don't worship the New Testament...nor do I think my goal in life is to follow the New Testament). Rather, my focus here is how one can be anti-authoritarian and still affirm discipleship and submission.

Let's tackle submission first. I'm a big fan of mutual submission (all of those one-another statements in the New Testament make it clear that our goal is interdependence and mutuality, not independence and individual freedom). To me, this shouldn't pose a problem for anarcho-communists or those groups who affirm consensus. After all, consensus is almost a structure for mutual submission. However, mutual submission goes deeper than consensus. Consensus recognizes the value of each voice. But, as the apostle Paul teaches regarding spiritual gifts and mutuality, sometimes we need to submit to the one in our midst who is clearly speaking a spirit-filled word.

Our goal isn't simply to all agree with one another. Rather, it is to discern the Spirit in our midst, and all agree together concerning the way in which the Spirit is moving.

And it is assumed that there are some who are wiser about discerning the Spirit–who have deeper practices in the way of Jesus. These folks are often considered elders and they can mentor folks just starting out in the way of Jesus. This is what discipleship is all about. Is it hierarchical? Perhaps, but if it is, it is a dynamic hierarchy rather than a static one. The goal of discipleship should never be to have permanent leaders. Rather, it should be to recognize wisdom where it is found, and to learn from that wisdom. Most anarchists do that.

Christian anarchists reject violence...

Not all Christian anarchists are pacifists. And not all "secular" anarchists reject nonviolence. Nevertheless, Christian anarchists tend towards pacifism. While some groups (like traditional Anabaptists) embrace a meeker pacifism of passive nonresistance, most Christian groups with an anarchic impulse support a more proactive nonviolence. Many Christian anarchists are nonviolent because Jesus challenged his followers to love their enemies and "turn the other cheek" when struck. For many (if not most) Christian anarchists, the anarchic vision begins with Jesus' loving mutuality that challenges social divisions and triumphs over the Powers.

Furthermore, many Christian anarchists are inspired by a future vision of shalom free from violence (even violence against non-human animals). And, since many also believe (a belief exemplified, perhaps, by the Quakers) that the Inner Light exists within all people, Christian anarchism tends to have a hopeful view of God's ability to transform all people.

To many anarchists, these items of faith are foolish distractions that, at best, make Christian anarchists dopey and irrelevant. At worst, Christian anarchists are pawns of oppression (folks like Ward Churchill and Peter Gelderloos have been particularly vocal in rejecting anarcho-pacifism).

To be fair, this tension exists apart from Christian anarchism, though most proponents of nonviolence have been influenced by those great modern figures who were, in turn, influenced by Jesus Christ (such as Tolstoy, Gandhi, and King).

To be honest, I'm not sure I see this tension ever being resolved. Perhaps the best way to live with each other in our shared hopes for a new world is for proponents of nonviolence to remain humble about their critique of revolutionary violence[37] while those who want to utilize a "diversity of tactics" should recognize the wisdom to be learned from nonviolent traditions.

It is also important, I think, to remember that Jesus' teachings aren't the same as Gandhi's. Many Christians have mistakenly assumed, based upon Jesus' life and teachings, that everything we usually identify as "violent" is off-limits. Yet clearly, Jesus engaged in such things as property destruction, verbal abuse, and civil disobedience. Rather than developing an absolutist code, we should engage Scripture in the midst of the practice of communal discernment in particular contexts and let things develop from there.

Christian anarchists don't resist the State...

Most anarchists are against structures like the State, whereas many Christian anarchists are merely indifferent to the State, advocating a sort of "Two Kingdoms" theology.

This is a subtle issue. Many traditional Anabaptists and many neo-Anabaptists hold the view that there are two kingdoms, each of which should be kept totally separate. The idea is that, once you become a Christian, you have nothing to do with the kingdom of the world, since you are now a part of the Kingdom of God. You can't be a

---

37 For a great article on this, see Nichola Torbett's "Confessing Pacifism, Repenting in Love" which was published by Jesus Radicals online at:
www.jesusradicals.com/confessing-pacifism-repenting-in-love

soldier or in the government. You shouldn't vote. But, if folks want to be soldiers or in the government or engage in oppression in that "other" kingdom—the kingdom of this world—that is their choice and we should leave them to it. We'll render to God what is God's and let Caesar go about his business.

This has led some folks (like Greg Boyd) to conclude that we shouldn't get involved with protesting. Many who have read Boyd and Yoder come to the conclusion that our prophetic witness is in being a Kingdom alternative, not in directly challenging the State (or, perhaps, other structures of oppression?).

I reject this line of thinking, as do many other Christian anarchists. I don't believe that our only witness results in pulling people out of oppressive structures into radical Christian community. I used to think that way, but I've found that you can't create a healthy alternative without also becoming adept at naming and engaging in acts of resistance against systems of oppression. Yes, there is a danger of simply getting sucked into the system with its ways of managing oppression. But if we are too afraid of getting our hands "dirty," we may simply end up with little farms and urban intentional communities that think they are free from taint, yet still (unwittingly) embodying the oppressiveness found in larger society within their own mini-societies. I find that naming oppression within myself requires naming oppression that I see in the world.

At least Christianity is diverse...

I am a white male. And so are a majority of self-described anarchists. However, most self-described Christians are neither white nor male. This is due to a whole host of reasons (having to do with the history of colonialism and the birth of early anarchism). This difference is probably worthy of its own book (by someone far better suited for addressing it than I). However, it remains that Christianity has found ways of sparking liberatory imagination among marginalized groups in ways that isn't exactly true of anarchism. This isn't because of the superiority of Christianity (history reveals that Christianity has been fairly inept at undoing oppressions). And it may be because 1 billion people are more likely to nurture pockets of diversity than thousands of anarchists are. Nevertheless, the diversity of Christian expressions provides more opportunities for people of color, older people, and non-males to have a voice.

It is challenging to find a place within anarchist circles if you aren't a white male. When you join Christianity and anarchism, it gets even harder to nurture a safe place. It is like combining the whiteness of anarchism with the heteronormativity and latent patriarchalism of Christianity. Which certainly gives us a great deal to work on here, doesn't it?

* * * * *

The challenge here, I think, is to recognize that it is fair to see Christian anarchism as both a part of the development of early anarchism as well as a unique tradition in its own right. Whether we like it or not, those who embrace Christian anarchism are going to find it difficult to really "fit in" with the mainstream anarchist crowd or with the mainstream Christian crowd.

The temptation is to try to force it. To try to show why our views fit "perfectly" within our theological traditions or to show anarchists how we're just like them (except that we pray). I don't think we should try too hard to fit in at all, rather, we should own our peculiarity and let it become our strength. Let us focus on how we can offer a unique perspective and give flesh to that perspective. Instead of trying to blend in, we should find a way to speak boldly and forge a path that seeks to be faithful to the way of Jesus in increasingly poignant ways.

Further Reading

Michael Bakunin, *God and the State*, Mineola, New York: Dover Publications, 1970.

Peter Gelderloos, *How Nonviolence Protects the State*, Cambridge, Massachusetts, South End Press, 2007.

6

The unKingdom of God is Here

There is a very real temptation, when exploring the intersection of Christianity and anarchism, to simply force one category into the other. I see this all the time.

There are those who simply believe that their Christian tradition is so inherently anarchistic that they can simply "claim" anarchism. They trump all other anarchisms in such a way as to dismiss them entirely. There is a danger in this: it creates theological ghettos increasingly unable to respond to current political and spiritual crises. Those who live in theological ghettos assume that everyone else should be like them. Meanwhile the world and its people continue to rush headlong towards the abyss.

And there are those who see Christianity as a useful tool on one's journey towards anarchism. They see anti-domination as their true god, and even Christ serves to bring people to this god. The danger of this temptation is that anything sacred becomes scrapped for parts to a cause that will never arrive. The inner transformation necessary for social liberation cannot be obtained simply through structural analysis. There is a reason Marx was never a Marxist. There is a reason why some of my most brilliantly anarchistic friends come off as authoritarian. There is simply more oppressing us than social structures. And more is required for us to embrace our fullest humanity than tearing down oppressive structures and replacing them with our clever utopias.

If one is a Christian *anarchist*, who largely congregates with other anarchists, then it could easily be understood that one's Christianity is simply their own flavor of anarchism. And, when it comes down to it, anarchism is what it's all about. Likewise, if one is a *Christian* anarchist, then one could easily feel that one's anarchism is simply a political affiliation...and that, being in fellowship with militaristic Capitalist patriotic Christians is more important than seeking liberation. Neither appeal to me.

The best way forward, it seems to me, is to be rooted in the particularity of the story of Jesus and the church. I assume—and I realize this is a big assumption—that Jesus shows us a bold new way to be human: a way that not only challenges domination, but also transforms us. It is more than political (but isn't less than political...it offers real insight in how we live together in communities of practice). But it is also more than spiritual (but it isn't less than spiritual...it offers real insight in how our hearts can be animated by the Spirit of God). The way of Jesus is integrated; the "unkingdom of God" confronts our political, economic, religious realities. It challenges both the social world and our interior spaces.

A Christian anarchism must be rooted in Jesus' vision. However, I don't believe we can really live into that vision without learning from sources outside of the Christian tradition. We can't bible-study our way past our imaginative impasse. Our tradition is so enmeshed within the story of imperialism that we must be open to external critiques of both imperialism and Christianity.

It is bad enough that our Christianity has fueled imperialism. If the story ended there, we could simply stop contributing to the imperial machine and try to fix things. Christianity not only injected some of its DNA into Empire (thus Christianizing empire), but empire has injected its DNA into Christianity, thus imperializing our Christianity. It is almost impossible to understand how deep the infection goes.

Ours is a faith that has, largely, worked in opposition to its Object. Christendom has, in its imperial journey, cast out much of its anti-imperial core like demons. The Gospel has been rendered Satanic and the Satanic has become the Gospel.

We need to relearn the Way of Jesus. And we need to develop practices to help us in this pedagogical task. If we simply retreat into the safe confines of traditional Christianity, we treat the living Christ as a dead man, one who left us timeless wisdom. Likewise, if we rush into anarchist critiques without a real sense of the mystical presence of Christ, we are simply tearing down the lego-castle of oppression and using those lego blocks to construct our utopias.

So then, how do we proceed? Do we simply smash Christianity and anarchism together into some sort of strained mashup? This is a more difficult task than it might seem at first. Many Christian anarchists have no idea how to put these two things together in any way that makes sense to them. They simply hold one tradition in each hand, ignoring the conflict they feel until, eventually, they let go of one of them.

I don't think of "Christian anarchism" as one subset of anarchism. Nor do I think of it as a subset of Christianity. Approaching things that way is helpful only to a point—because, in the end, it renders being either Christian or anarchist into an "optional" addition to one's primary identity. We need to resist the temptation to see Christian anarchism as a category of people...or as a faction.

Christian anarchism is perhaps better understood as an interpretation, a way of understanding the "unkingdom of God."

Or we may see Christian anarchism as a dialogue about the shape of revolutionary practice. This follows the logic of David Graeber in *Fragments of an Anarchist Anthropology*, where he suggests, "anarchism has tended to be an ethical discourse about revolutionary practice" rather than a theory-driven endeavor.

THE PARTICULARITY OF CHRISTIAN ANARCHISM

Language will always fail to describe the strange relationship between the Way of Jesus and anarchistic political impulses. There are some real downsides to identifying as a "Christian anarchist." The stress naturally falls on one of the two words as though they are two separate things smashed together, unreconcilable into any cohesive whole.

I've toyed with alternative language: anarcho-Christianity, Christarchy, Christianarchy, Christo-anarchy, etc. All of these get at an important truth, but fail to resolve the tension without over-emphasizing one aspect.[38] Even my own affinity for a phrase like the "unkingdom of God" is often too confusing to be helpful in polite conversation.[39] Because fresh names allow for greater definitional freedom, I have taken to using the phrase "Christo-

---

38 For example, "Christarchy" signifies the reign of Christ, but doesn't qualify the nature of that reign as, basically, an un-reign. "Christianarchy" sounds like the reign of Christians. "Anarcho-Christianity" or "Christo-anarchy" come closest to creating an appropriately blurry tension, but each stresses one part of the equation more than the other. None, in reality, evoke a new imagination—drawing us to a way of thinking that moves beyond classical anarchism or traditional mainstream Christianity.

39 I recognize that the best conversations are neither polite nor free from confusion

anarchism."[40] Nevertheless, the "name" isn't as important as the perspective it signifies:

> Christo-anarchism refers not only to the insight that Jesus' vision of the [un]Kingdom of God has anarchic (anti-domination) implications, but also the assumption that, only by nurturing practices centered on the presence of the Living Christ, can we move from domination to non-domination, from death to life, from oppression to liberation, and from alienation to love.

This is my suggestion of a starting point for thinking about Christo-anarchism. To me, this "definition" (I'm reluctant to call it a definition) addresses several important concerns:

1) It doesn't diminish that there are practical anarchic implications to Jesus' vision. This opens up space to learn from other anarchistic groups and discerningly adopt their practices *as an expression* of Jesus' vision. This allows us to dialogue and learn from "secular" anarchists in a way that focuses on shared commitments to anti-domination. Working together doesn't depend upon having a shared theology or shared spirituality.

2) It centers practice on the Risen Christ, rather than on abstracted principles gleaned from Scripture. This places Christo-anarchism clearly into the realm of mystical anarchism, rather than merely "materialist" anarchism (though I realize that it is possible to be both a materialist and a mystic).

---

40 I choose "Christo-anarchism" for several reasons. Firstly, it corresponds and subverts the ideology that Dorothee Soelle's has named "Christo-fascism." Secondly, it emphasizes Christ rather than Christianity. Thirdly, Christo-anarchism suggests "anarchism in the way of Jesus".

3) The emphasis is on nurturing practices. Most anarchists recognize that our practices today should point to the future we long for (this is called "prefigurative politics"). Likewise, whatever practice we employ should embody a Christo-anarchist politics. However, they should be accessible to other Christians, thus building a bridge with other Christian groups who don't share our analysis. Much like anarchists contributed to group processes for the Occupy Movement, Christo-anarchists can share practices with the larger Body of Christ even if they don't affirm the rationale for these practices.

4) The goal here is process and movement, not in developing an ideological utopia. There is a real tendency to "blueprint" our utopian communities. That is, we use our imaginations to think of an ideal community or approach and then attempt to create it, often stepping on people along the way. Our emphasis should be on being transformed as well as in transforming. We should discern together, step by step, as we come to learn Jesus' fresh vision for our communities. It isn't sufficient to engage in Biblical hermeneutics, extract Biblical principles, and then attempt to bring them to life by enforcing them into a community. Our current social, political, and spiritual crises aren't due to a lack of utopic visions. Nor is it a failure of biblical interpretation. Rather, it is a failure of discernment.[41]

MYSTICAL CHRISTO-ANARCHIST PRACTICES

I'm going to resist the temptation to lay out a string of the

---

41 Indeed, when Paul issued his challenge to Corinth (1 Cor. 11:29) over the injustices around the Lord's Supper, the core failure wasn't simply a lack of analysis. No, he saw it as a failure in "discerning the body of Christ." One can have the right analysis and still fail to see things for what they are.

usual anarchist practices. I've already named the tendency to "blueprint" our utopian visions. It would be über-lame of me to name that tendency only to proceed to lay out a blueprint. However, I do have some suggestions for practices (perhaps they could be considered meta-practices) that will help us to discern the shape and practice of Christo-anarchism in our own particular contexts.

We need practices that help us learn the way of Jesus, not just practices that help us implement the way of Jesus. It's not just about doing good in this world; it is part of our imperial training for us to assume that we know what is good...what is best...and to then force the world to conform to that vision. Rather, these practices are about helping us see the world differently and then acting in that world in a way that is transformative.[42] Our most pressing need is for practices that help us see the world through a different lens than that of imperial myth and civilizational programming.

To me, this is a mystical endeavor. Mysticism, as I understand it, is direct encounter with the Divine. It isn't a disembodied experience; it is deeply tangible. In our world, we experience separation and alienation from God, from one another, and from the land beneath our feet. Mysticism isn't an escape from these realities; it is seeing what is real. Any time we experience the demolishing of

---

42 I'm trying to use the word "transform" in the Freirean sense: "[T]he more radical the person is, the more fully he or she enters into reality so that, knowing it better, he or she can transform it. This individual is not afraid to confront, to listen, to see the world unveiled. This person is not afraid to meet the people or to enter into a dialogue with them. This person does not consider himself or herself the proprietor of history or of all people, or the liberator of the oppressed; but he or she does commit himself or herself, within history, to fight at their side." - Paulo Freire, *Pedagogy of the Oppressed* (New York: Continuum, 2000), p. 39

the walls of separation–when we feel the presence of God, when we meaningfully and truly connect with one another in human relationships, when we feel as though we are an integral part of creation along with the trees and the soil and the daffodils and nonhuman animals–it is a mystical moment. To be mystics is to experience reality. And the goal of anarchists of all varieties is to reject that which is unreal–the principalities and powers (the abstract structures that manage creation and humanity)–and to live the way humanity is suppose to live.

I offer, then, these practices as a starting point. They aren't even remotely exhaustive. But I am convinced they are excellent places to begin our journey to see the inbreaking of the unKingdom of God in our midst:

1) We need to tell the stories of the places in which we live from the vantage point of the oppressed. If we are going to develop practices that show love to one another and to the land under our feet, we need to embrace the confessional practice of truth-telling. I live in Minneapolis. It isn't far from the place the Dakota believe is the source of the Dakota people. Minneapolis began as an occupation. Fort Snelling was built upon what many of us might see as the Dakota "Garden of Eden" in order to break the spirits of a people. It was a staging ground for assaults against the Dakota. Many were forced into camps there and shipped to other places in the United States. Many died in these camps. There is, of course, much more to this story. But, the more I tell the untold story of this place, the less that the civilizational myths (that Minnesota was born in the mid 1800s as settlers came and made the land productive, eventually creating the State of Minnesota–the 32nd territory to join the United States, etc) hold power over my imagination.

2) We need to honestly tell the story of how we relate to the places in which we live. If I am going to come to terms

with the domination in my own heart, I need to explore my identity in relationship to the place in which I live. This is the only way I can begin to break the "spell" over my imagination that sees myself as an American citizen, or as an individual consumer, or as a thing called a "white man." By telling the stories of our places and telling our own stories, we can can work through the layers of conditioning and myth and propaganda. We can begin, slowly, to relate to each other in truth.

3) We need to experiment towards a gift economy. Simone Weil believed that money was the single greatest contributing factor in creating uprootedness (the experience of alienation from place, people, and God). As communities, we need to explore different ways of living outside of currency transactions. This is not only a good practice in general (for issues of justice), but it is a mystical practice. The use of money reinforces a great number of myths in our society–it keeps us from seeing things as they are, and instead shapes a worldview that sees relationships as transactional and creation as a set of commodities. As Christians, our gift economy should be rooted in our practice of the Lord's Supper, where we discern the Body and practice Jubilee.

4) We should develop practices of silence and communal discernment. The Quakers are onto something important. Spiritual discernment that allows for silence is beautiful and necessary. Long-time Quakers will tell you that their communal discernment practices are far from perfect. But they offer a way into a life of discernment. I'm not simply talking about consensus-based decision making (which is important, to be sure). Rather, I am talking about discernment: hearing God and one another in a shared space. Decision-making need not be the goal. We need to listen to the Holy Spirit, rather than simply reading about how the Holy Spirit communicated to dead Apostles. In a

noisy world of over-information, communal discernment is more essential than ever.

5) We must enter into real relationships with the marginalized. And if we consider ourselves among the marginalized, we should develop relationships with other marginalized people in our places. This is the idea behind Segundo Galilea's "integral liberation": Humans are not able to find true compassion, nor create structures of deep transformation, without entering into Jesus' own compassion, which is incarnate in the poor and marginalized. Being "aware" of social injustice doesn't collapse the alienation experienced between human beings. We must nurture real relationships, relatively free from agenda, before we develop strong conclusions about what justice looks like.

* * * * *

This is, of course, a small beginning. But I can only begin with those practices that have helped me see the world differently. They are process-oriented practices that, in and of themselves, aren't particularly utopian (though they are still prefigurative). However, they are practices that can help us discern and develop concreted practices for the places we inhabit.

My hope in this final chapter was to express a shift: a shift away from seeing Christian anarchism as a set of beliefs and ideals, as well as a shift away from seeing it as a category or a faction. Rather, I want to see it as a way of *interpreting* and as a *set of practices* first and foremost. Certainly, likeminded communities are bound to network and organize around common ideals and convictions. This is important and good. But in that networking and organizing, I believe our focus should be on engaging the Living Christ.

As a friend of mine once told me: "All we have to offer the world is the Presence of God." I agree. I believe that this Presence tears down walls of alienation. And that is, in so many important ways, an anarchist project.

www.ingramcontent.com/pod-product-compliance
Lightning Source LLC
Chambersburg PA
CBHW020603030426
42337CB00013B/1198